Your Future as a
PLUMBER

Your Future as a
PLUMBER

RACHEL GIVEN-WILSON AND SIMONE PAYMENT

Rosen
YA™

New York

Published in 2020 by The Rosen Publishing Group, Inc.
29 East 21st Street, New York, NY 10010

Library of Congress Cataloging-in-Publication Data

Names: Given-Wilson, Rachel, author. | Payment, Simone, author.
Title: Your future as a plumber / Rachel Given-Wilson and Simone Payment.
Description: First edition. | New York, NY : The Rosen Publishing
Group, Inc., 2020. | Series: High-demand careers | Includes
bibliographical references and index. | Audience: Grades 7–12.
Identifiers: LCCN 2018050602| ISBN 9781508187899
(library bound) | ISBN 9781508187882 (pbk.)
Subjects: LCSH: Plumbing—Vocational guidance—Juvenile literature.
Classification: LCC TH6130 .G58 2020 | DDC 696/.1023—dc23
LC record available at https://lccn.loc.gov/2018050602

Manufactured in China

Contents

Introduction   6

Chapter 1
WHAT DOES IT TAKE TO BE A PLUMBER?   9

Chapter 2
GENERAL PLUMBERS   24

Chapter 3
PIPE FITTERS, PIPELAYERS, STEAMFITTERS, AND
SPRINKLER FITTERS   37

Chapter 4
MASTER PLUMBERS AND BUSINESS OWNERS   45

Chapter 5
THE FUTURE OF PLUMBING   57

GLOSSARY   67
FOR MORE INFORMATION   69
FOR FURTHER READING   73
BIBLIOGRAPHY   74
INDEX   77

People all over the world rely on plumbers. Plumbers are responsible for providing many of the conveniences of modern living. They hook up kitchen faucets, allowing people to have a cold glass of water on a hot day. They install water heaters that heat the water to fill the bathtub on a chilly night. Plumbers also install the dishwashers in school cafeterias and the washing machines at the local laundromat. Many people take these things for granted, but they would not be available without the hard work of plumbers.

If you're somebody who enjoys figuring out what the problem is and fixing things, a career as a plumber may be perfect for you. It's a job that is always in demand!

Plumbing can be a great career for people who get satisfaction out of building and fixing things. Hattie Hasan of Leeds, in the United Kingdom, decided to become a plumber and start her own plumbing company in 1990. "I looked around at my life and what I love doing. Fixing things, being a hero, and my passion for water all took me towards plumbing," she told AutoStraddle in a 2016 interview. Hasan started out by buying her own secondhand tools and a telephone answering machine (in the days before cell phones) and posting flyers advertising her services. Her company, Stopcocks, now has plumbers in cities all over the United Kingdom.

Fred Schilling is a master plumber and the founder and chief operating officer of Pipeline Plumbing in South Florida. He got his training while he was in the Air Force and went on to became one of the youngest certified master plumbers in the country, at the age of twenty-five. He loves his job but says it's hard work because plumbers always have to be on call. In an interview in *Lifehacker*, Schilling discusses the sense of accomplishment and pride he feels when he sees one of the thousands of buildings he has helped to construct over the years.

Plumbing can be a great career to pursue because plumbers are always in demand. When the economy is bad, people might choose to save money by putting off building a new home. However, it is unlikely that they'll wait to fix a broken sink or toilet.

According to 2018 data from the Bureau of Labor Statistics, employment of plumbers, pipe fitters, and steamfitters was projected to grow 16 percent between 2016 and 2026. This demand will be due partly to new construction and the ongoing need to repair and maintain systems in existing buildings. In addition, some states are beginning to require sprinkler systems to be installed in residential and other buildings, leading to an increased need for plumbers who specialize in sprinkler fitting.

If you're interested in a career as a plumber, now is a great time to be starting to plan your future. Even if you're still in high school, there are classes you can take and projects you can work on to begin honing your plumbing skills now!

Chapter 1

WHAT DOES IT TAKE TO BE A PLUMBER?

*P*lumbers install and repair pipes carrying liquids or gases to and from all kinds of buildings, including homes, offices, schools, and factories. Some plumbers choose to specialize in a specific area, such as pipe fitting and steamfitting. However, all plumbers need to be trained in the basic skills required in the plumbing industry. Aspiring plumbers have a few different options when it comes to learning the trade and getting qualified.

GENERAL STATISTICS

According to 2018 data from the Bureau of Labor Statistics, there are almost half a million plumbers, pipe fitters, and steamfitters in the United States. Sixty-two percent of them work for contractors. Plumbers who work for contractors may install plumbing in new homes or buildings, or they might fix or update existing plumbing. Other plumbers work outside of the construction industry. For example, they might work on a natural gas pipeline or for the oil industry. About 13 percent of all plumbers are self-employed.

In general, plumbers make the highest salary of all the jobs in the construction industry. Of course, not all plumbers make the same salary. Their pay can vary depending on where they work, the tasks they perform, and their level of expertise.

TYPES OF JOBS

Many plumbers work on new construction projects. Some work on residential structures, such as new houses, high-rise apartment buildings, or college dorms. They also might work on commercial structures, such as baseball stadiums, shopping malls, or restaurants. Each kind of new building requires its own specific plumbing system. Some kinds of buildings, such as fire stations, scientific laboratories, and hospitals, might have special plumbing needs.

Plumbers are also called upon to install fixtures like bathtubs, showers, and toilets. Fixtures are devices that are attached to a wall or floor. Plumbing fixtures use water and usually have a pipe bringing water in and a

Plumbers need to know how to install fixtures such as bathtubs, toilets, and showers. These fixtures must be set up properly so that the water flows and drains without a problem.

drain to let water out. Plumbers also install appliances that use water but are not necessarily attached to the wall or floor, such as dishwashers, hot water heaters, and washing machines.

In addition to putting in fixtures and appliances, plumbers install gas lines for stoves and heating systems. They install all the pipes that bring the water to the kitchen and bath fixtures, as well as the pipes that take water away from them to sewer lines or septic tanks. Plumbers also fix and maintain the pipes and fixtures they install. They may work on remodeling projects in kitchens or bathrooms, or they might update the plumbing in an existing home to accommodate the homeowner's needs. For instance, if a couple decides that they want to heat their home with natural gas instead of oil, they will hire a plumber to run a new gas line into the home.

A plumber may specialize in a particular type of work. However, most plumbers know how to do many types of jobs. They might do several different types of job over the course of a week or even during a single workday.

GETTING THE RIGHT EDUCATION

There are several different paths to becoming a plumber. Students who already know they would like to become a plumber have a number of options. After high school, they can go straight to work as an apprentice plumber, or they can go to college or attend a trade school before becoming an apprentice plumber. Some people work in another career before deciding to become a plumber. For instance, they might work for several years as a pipe fitter before deciding to become a plumber. Some people become plumbers after spending time in a completely unrelated career as well.

HIGH SCHOOL CLASSES

It's never too soon for junior high or high school students to begin preparing themselves for a career in plumbing. Professional plumbers need to have good math skills to do their job. Taking math classes, especially algebra and

High school science classes are a good way to prepare for a career as a plumber. A solid understanding of physics and chemistry helps students understand the science of plumbing.

geometry, can be an especially good way to prepare for this career. Because plumbers often work with a variety of materials, science classes like physics and chemistry are also useful. Alongside these academic courses, it is a good idea to take classes in drafting and mechanical drawing. Technical education classes can teach students how to properly use a variety of tools, as well as the fundamentals of skills such as welding.

VOCATIONAL SCHOOLS

Students who are interested in pursuing a career in plumbing may choose to go to vocational school, rather than the last year or two of high school. Vocational schools (which are also sometimes called trade schools) provide students with the skills and training needed for a particular career, such as car repair, carpentry, and plumbing.

However, they also offer students many of the same kinds of classes they would take in high school, such as English or history. Students interested in attending a vocational school should talk to their school guidance counselor for more information. If there is a vocational school nearby, students can arrange a visit to learn more.

TECHNICAL SCHOOL AND COMMUNITY COLLEGE

After graduating from vocational school or high school, people who want to become plumbers may choose to attend community college or a technical school. Technical schools are similar to vocational schools. They also teach

Job Corps

The US Department of Labor runs a program called Job Corps for teens and young adults. The Job Corps offers courses in several construction trades, including plumbing. The program also helps teens and young adults ages sixteen to twenty-four earn their high school diploma or General Educational Development (GED) diploma. Once students have completed the program, Job Corps helps them create résumés and find employment. An excellent option for those who are having a difficult time affording college, this program is free to anyone who qualifies for it. To find out more or apply for Job Corps, visit the website, www.jobcorps.gov.

particular skills that will help prepare a student for a future career. Technical school programs are usually two years long. Some community colleges offer skill-specific classes as well. At most community colleges, you can get an associate's degree after two years or a bachelor's degree after four years.

At community college or technical school, students can learn how to read plumbing blueprints. They will also begin learning about specific plumbing codes. In addition, students will learn special skills, such as welding. Perhaps most importantly, students can take safety classes so that they know how to stay safe on the job.

MAKING THE RIGHT CHOICE

Attending a vocational school, technical school, or community college is not a requirement for becoming a plumber. Some plumbers leave high school and immediately enter an apprenticeship. This involves starting work as an apprentice plumber and taking classes at night or on weekends. When it comes to deciding whether to go to college or not, there is no right or wrong answer. A student's choice may depend on his or her personality, financial situation, or goals. There are benefits and drawbacks to each choice. When making the decision, students should carefully weigh their options.

An advantage of continuing to community college or technical school is that students can learn from experts. Teachers are available to answer questions. Students are also part of a

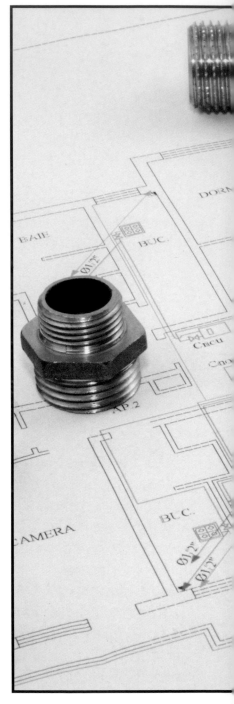

Learning to read a bluepint is one of the most important skills plumbers around the world need to have. A bluprint is a detailed plan showing how each part of a construction project fits together.

community and can discuss what they're learning with their classmates. By working together, students at a community college can have a richer learning experience than they might have had trying to figure things out by themselves. Students interested in owning their own plumbing business some day can take accounting and business management classes while at community college. Another advantage of school is that students can take classes in specialized topics relevant to plumbing. These classes give students a head start when they begin an apprenticeship program.

A disadvantage of community college or technical school is that it costs money. Students will most likely not be able to work a full-time job while attending college and will have to work around their class schedule. However, many schools offer scholarships, grants, and other forms of financial aid that can help defray the cost of tuition.

Some high school or vocational school graduates decide to begin an apprenticeship program. One advantage of doing an apprenticeship program is that apprentices earn a regular salary. More important, they also get hands-on experience working with professional plumbers. Apprentices also create their own study schedule on nights or weekends.

Students who want more help with the decision of whether to apply to school or begin working should speak with their school guidance counselor. A guidance counselor can not only provide students with valuable career advice, but can also help them find information about community colleges, trade schools, and apprenticeship programs.

APPRENTICESHIP PROGRAMS

During an apprenticeship program, the real work of being a plumber begins. An apprenticeship consists of getting actual, hands-on experience by working alongside an experienced plumber, known as a master plumber. During this time, apprentices learn everything they will need to know to become a licensed plumber.

WHAT IS AN APPRENTICESHIP PROGRAM?

Apprenticeships are on-the-job training programs. In addition to working with experienced plumbers, apprentices also take classes at night or on weekends. In some apprenticeship programs, apprentices work four days a week and attend classes one day a week. Most apprenticeship programs last four or five years. Each year, apprentices are expected to spend about two thousand hours working and about one hundred and fifty to two hundred hours taking classes. Apprenticeship programs vary from state to state and from program to program.

Working with a master plumber, apprentices learn to read blueprints and building plans so that they will know where to place pipes. They become familiar with the varieties of pipes and other plumbing materials, study building codes and become familiar with important safety procedures, and learn how to use all the tools needed to get the job done.

An apprenticeship program is a great way to learn a trade like plumbing. Apprentices learn from experienced plumbers while working alongside them.

REQUIREMENTS FOR APPRENTICESHIP PROGRAMS

Apprentices must be at least eighteen years old and in good physical condition. In many cases, apprentices must have graduated from high school or have a GED. Apprenticeship programs often require that apprentices have a driver's license, and many programs require that apprentices pass a drug test. A birth certificate, or another document that proves that applicants are eighteen or older, as well as documentation proving that the applicant is a citizen or legal immigrant is sometimes requested.

Apprenticeships are generally run by unions or contractor organizations. Here is a list of organizations that sponsor plumbing apprenticeships:

- ☼ American Fire Sprinkler Association
- ☼ Associated Builders and Contractors

◘ Home Builders Institute of the National Association of Home Builders
◘ Mechanical Contractors Association of America
◘ National Fire Sprinkler Association
◘ Plumbing-Heating-Cooling Contractors Association
◘ United Association of Journeymen and Apprentices of the Plumbing and Pipe Fitting Industry of the United States and Canada

To find a local apprenticeship, students can check with one of these organizations or with their state's employment and training office.

In addition to on-the-job training, apprentices spend time in the classroom. There they learn more about math, science, safety, first aid, many types of plumber's tools, various pipe systems, and many other topics. They also learn how to weld, how to work with natural gas, and how to read blueprints and plans. The course requirements for a plumber's apprentice can vary by state.

WAGES AND BENEFITS

Apprentice plumbers usually make about half the salary of what experienced plumbers earn. As apprentices gain more experience, their wages go up. The kind of benefits they receive, such as health insurance, depend on the union they belong to or their employer. Apprentices usually receive benefits such as health insurance, as well as pensions and retirement savings plans.

OTHER THINGS LEARNED DURING AN APPRENTICESHIP

Apprentices learn more than just plumbing skills from the plumbers who train them. For example, if they work in residential plumbing, apprentices will learn good communication skills and how to work well with customers. Plumbers who own their own businesses might also teach apprentices how to run their own companies someday. If apprentices work in commercial plumbing, they'll learn to work on a team with other contractors. For example, commercial plumbers might need to interact with electricians, elevator installers, and heating or air-conditioning technicians.

Chapter 2

GENERAL PLUMBERS

*P*lumbing is a highly skilled job that involves a range of responsibilities, from reading blueprints and following state building codes to choosing the right materials for the job. Although some plumbers go on to specialize in certain areas, it's important for all plumbers to have a well-rounded training and a strong understanding of the basic skills required for general pluming.

THE WORK OF A PLUMBER

Most plumbers work a regular workweek. That means they work Monday through Friday, from about 9:00 AM to 5:00 PM. However, some plumbers work for twenty-four-hour repair services. These plumbers are "on call." This means they must be available to fix an emergency, such as a burst pipe.

In the past, large buildings, power plants, and manufacturing plants often had full-time plumbers on staff. Now it is more common for such places to rely on outside companies for their plumbing needs. Therefore, more plumbers today work for twenty-four-hour repair services than in the past.

A plumber's workload is usually steady, although he or she may be busier at certain times of the year than others. New construction generally occurs in the spring through fall in most parts of the country, so there is usually more work available for plumbers during this time. Plumbers may

When a pipe bursts, it's time to call a plumber! This type of emergency is more likely to occur during the winter months, when the water inside the pipes may freeze and expand.

work on indoor remodeling projects during the winter and might also be called upon to perform repair work on heating systems or to mend burst pipes.

Sometimes a plumber will work on a big, temporary project. For example, a plumber might work on the construction of a new hospital. When the project is done, the plumber might be out of work until his or her next project starts. Most of the time, however, successful plumbers go right from one project to the next.

Being a plumber can be a dirty job. When doing indoor work, plumbers often have to operate in dusty or dirty buildings or in small, cramped spaces. Outdoors, plumbers must often work in difficult weather conditions. They must be careful to observe the proper safety practices while at the work site, as many work sites can be dangerous if workers are not careful. To avoid injury, plumbers need to be aware of the danger posed by saws and sharp pipes. They must also be careful to avoid getting burned while using welding torches or working on steam pipes and to avoid falls when working on ladders or scaffolding.

Plumbers are often called to fix blockages in sinks, toilets, and bathtubs. They need to know which tools to use for different types of blockages.

Plumbers perform many jobs. The two main tasks of plumbers are installation and repair. Plumbers install new pipes and pipe systems. On residential jobs, plumbers may install plumbing and appliances. When plumbers work on commercial jobs, they may also install specialized equipment. For example, a plumber might install a special pipe system in a laboratory that uses hazardous chemicals.

The other main task plumbers perform is repair. They find and fix leaks in pipes, faucets, and water lines. They unclog pipes and drains. During the winter, plumbers may also repair damaged pipes. Cold temperatures can cause the water inside pipes to freeze and therefore expand, bursting the pipe. Over time, some types of pipe can also crack, causing serious leaks.

Sometimes plumbers are called upon to "rescue" things that have accidentally gone down a drain, such as rings or other jewelry. In some cases, plumbers use a cable with a small camera attached to locate the object. When the plumber finds the item, he or she can sometimes grab it with small pincers and pull it out. Other times, the fixture must be taken off the floor or wall in order to locate the missing object.

AN EXAMPLE OF A JOB FROM START TO FINISH

When starting a residential job on a house under construction, the first thing a plumber does is look over the blueprints and building plans from the architect and contractor. The plans tell the plumber where the fixtures will go. The plumber makes note of where the water line will come in from the street. He or she will also note where the sewage line, which connects the house to the municipal sewage system or a septic tank, will go.

The Things People Flush Down the Toilet

Most plumbers have their fair share of funny stories about things they've had to retrieve from blocked toilets. Steve Ferguson, the owner of Mr. Rooter Plumbing in Oakland and Berkeley, California, shared the following anecdote with *Popular Mechanics* for an article titled "7 Nightmarish Plumber Horror Stories": "One time we had an upstairs toilet clog job, which we ended up clearing by going through the pipes from the roof. To our surprise, we pulled back a dead raccoon from the drain through a 4-inch plumbing vent stack."

Plumber Ed Ernest had to deal with an even more delicate plumbing operation, which turned into a rescue, when he was called out to fix a mysterious toilet blockage and discovered a squirrel's tail sticking out of the toilet bowl. Andrew Olexiuk reported in *Absolute Draining and Plumbing*:

> He tried to pull on the tail, but the squirrel, against all odds, was still alive! Knowing he needed to be careful, and quick, he removed the toilet from the home's water supply in its entirety. This was the easiest step.
>
> After disconnecting the water, Ed found the water-logged squirrel poking its head out of the other end of the pipe. He took out his auger and, with some care and precision, he managed to get the head and two front paws of the poor squirrel out of the other end of the toilet. Grabbing the squirrel by the paws, Ed pulled him out completely. The poor thing was in shock but still alive, so Ed took it outside and put it on a nearby tree. In the end, the toilet *and the squirrel* were saved.

Based on the plans, the plumber will begin to lay out where the pipes will need to be placed. Once the pipes are roughly laid out, the plumber marks on the walls, ceilings, or floors where the pipes will go. He or she notes obstacles the pipes will need to go around, such as lines for electricity. The plumber then takes careful measurements so that he or she will have pipes of the correct length. The plumber must also make sure that installing pipes will not cause any other problems with the building. For instance, if the pipes are too heavy, they could pull away from their support and damage a wall or ceiling. Some appliances, such as washing machines, bathtubs or showers, need several pipes. These fixtures need separate pipes for hot and cold water and a pipe to drain away wastewater. The plumber will also need to make sure that the plumbing in the house conforms to local building codes.

When all marking and measuring is complete, the plumber begins cutting holes in walls, floors, or ceilings. The holes will allow the pipes to be attached to fixtures.

Plumbers need to take careful measurements to figure out exactly where the pipes should be placed. This requires a solid understanding of math.

After holes have been cut for every pipe, the plumber begins putting the pipes in place. Sometimes pipes must be hung using metal supports, and other times they are laid underground.

With the straight pipes in place, the plumber begins hooking them together with connectors. Connectors can be U-shaped, or they can be bent at an angle. This type of connector can connect a horizontal pipe to a vertical pipe. If a plumber is using metal pipes, sometimes he or she can bend them into the correct angle. Once the pipes are correctly connected, the plumber can begin to securely attach the pipes to each other. Pipes are attached using a number of different methods.

The next step is to attach the fixtures to the pipes. How the fixtures are attached depends on the fixture and the type of pipe being used. When all the pipes are attached to fixtures, the plumber begins testing all parts of the system. He or she turns all faucets on and off to make sure water is flowing and draining correctly. The plumber also checks the water pressure to make sure water is getting through pipes at the correct rate. If water is flowing too slowly or too quickly, the plumber must make adjustments.

Finally, a plumber must also set up a system of traps and vents. Traps are attached to the pipe that drains water away from a fixture, such as a sink. The trap holds a little of the water inside, which prevents gas from the sewer from coming up into the house or building. Vents go outside the building—usually through a roof—to allow air into the plumbing system. The air helps keep water flowing correctly.

A new residential construction job can last from several days to a week or more. The length of the job depends on the size of the house, how many fixtures must be installed, and how many bathrooms are in the house. The time needed can increase if the plumber discovers any problems in the construction or if he or she runs into difficulties with municipal water, gas, or sewer pipes.

GETTING A PLUMBING LICENSE

Getting a license is an important step for a plumber. Licensed plumbers not only make a higher salary, but they also supervise unlicensed plumbers on a jobsite. Plumbers can take their licensing exam once they've finished their apprenticeship.

Licensing exams vary from one place to another. To get a license, a plumber must pass a test on a variety of plumbing skills, as well as the local plumbing codes. In most places, there are two different tests: one for a journeyperson and one for a master plumber. Journeyperson licenses are for people who have finished their apprenticeships and have worked as a plumber for a certain number of years. Master licenses are for plumbers who already have a journeyperson license and have also worked for a required number of hours and taken additional night or weekend classes.

In addition to licenses for journeypersons and master plumbers, some states also have an additional license called a residential license. This license is for plumbers who have finished an apprenticeship but have not worked for as many years as a journeyperson.

There's a lot to learn when it comes to plumbing, but once you get your plumbing license, you'll be able to earn a higher salary and supervise other plumbers at the worksite.

It isn't possible for a plumber to get certified nationally. Instead, each state or local town has different licensing requirements and exams. Plumbers must be familiar with their state and local plumbing codes. If a plumber moves to a different state or city, he or she must get a new license to work in the area.

Licensing exams are usually made up of multiple choice, true or false, and fill-in-the-blank questions. These tests have questions on topics such as:

◘ Local plumbing codes
◘ Typical plumbing fixtures used in homes
◘ Specialized fixtures, such as large dishwashers used in restaurants
◘ The procedure for connecting a building to a public sewage system
◘ Types of pipe to use for particular jobs

Licensing exams can be difficult, and it is not unusual for someone to fail the test the first time. However, anyone who studies hard can eventually pass the test. Libraries and bookstores carry test preparation books that can help plumbers pass the exam, and there are plenty of online resources as well. In addition, many colleges and trade schools offer test preparation classes that can also help. These classes are usually held on nights and weekends. However, taking a class isn't always necessary—plumbers can also study on their own for the exam. Public libraries sometimes have online practice tests or classes that plumbers can take. Some plumbers choose to study with another plumber who is also preparing to take the licensing exam or get help from plumbers who have already passed the exam.

Chapter 3

PIPE FITTERS, PIPELAYERS, STEAMFITTERS, AND SPRINKLER FITTERS

Some plumbers choose to pursue a related career as a pipe fitter, pipelayer, steamfitter, or sprinkler fitter. These four careers have qualifications and career paths that are similar to general plumbing. Pipe fitters and pipelayers often work closely with plumbers.

PIPELAYERS

Pipelayers prepare the area where pipes will go. A pipelayer may dig a trench for a pipe by hand, using a shovel, or by using a backhoe or other digging equipment. Once the trench is dug, pipelayers position the pipe in the trench.

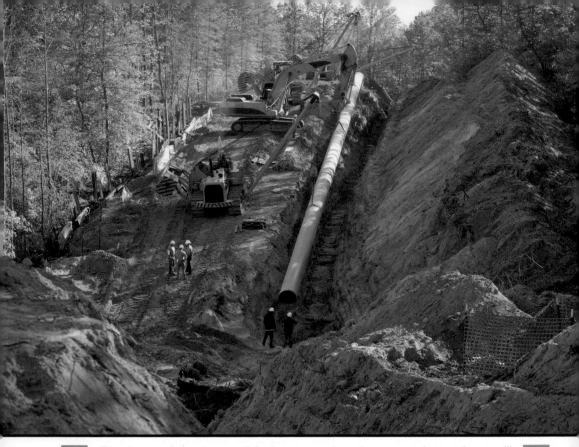

Pipelayers are responsible for preparing the area where pipes will go. This often involves digging a trench. When the area is ready, they lay the pipes in position.

When the pipe is in position, the pipelayer attaches the pieces of pipe together. Depending on the pipe material, he or she may use cement or glue, or pipelayers may weld it together.

Pipelayers most often work outside. Sometimes they work in remote areas or under difficult weather conditions. Like pipe fitters, they might work for a company that builds or maintains pipe systems in various locations. Other pipelayers might work for an employer in one location. For example, they might work for a city or town public works department. They could be called upon to lay pipes for a municipal water system or for other public utilities.

What's It Like to Be a Pipe Fitter?

Peter is a pipe fitter who works at Ingalls Shipbuilding in Pascagoula, Mississippi. In an interview with Dr. Kit Career Videos, he discussed his career path and daily tasks and offered advice to young people who are interested in pursuing a career as a pipe fitter.

Peter learned the pipe fitting trade as an apprentice for Ingalls and continues to work with the company. "The best part of the job to me is that I can finish the job and feel a sense of accomplishment." Peter also enjoys that he doesn't have to stay in one place. He has the chance to move around because there's a lot of opportunity to advance within the company. The worst parts of the job, he says, are waking up very early in the morning and having to work in all weather conditions.

Peter advises young people who are interested in a pipe fitting career to focus on math in school, particularly fractions. He also says it's important to be in good physical shape. "There's a lot of heavy lifting that can come into play on the pipe fitting job on a daily basis." Overall, Peter recommends pipe fitting as a great career for anyone who is prepared to work hard and really learn the trade.

PIPE FITTERS

Pipe fitters install and fix systems of pipes in buildings. They may install pipes that are part of a building's heating system, or they might work on pipe systems that are part

Sprinkler systems are installed by sprinkler fitters. These systems are usually found in offices, schools, and factories, but some apartment buildings also have them.

of a plant that manufactures chemicals, drugs, or other products. Pipe fitters also set up the controls that monitor pipe systems. These control systems can start or stop the flow of liquids or steam through the pipes and can turn on the timers and other mechanisms that start or stop the flow of fluids or gas automatically.

Like some plumbers, pipe fitters may work full time in one particular building. In general, however, pipe fitters are employed by companies that build or maintain pipe systems. In this capacity, pipe fitters might need to travel as part of their job. Pipe fitters might also work for a town or city water department. Because they often work on multistory buildings that are still under construction, pipe fitters must not be afraid of heights. Some pipe fitters specialize in using one type of pipe material or one type of pipe system. For example, a pipe fitter might specialize in working with pipes that carry chemicals. Others work on all kinds of pipes and pipe systems.

STEAMFITTERS

The duties of a steamfitter are similar to those of a pipe fitter. Steamfitters put in pipe systems, just as pipe fitters do. The difference is that the pipes that steamfitters install are used to move water or gas that is under pressure. For that reason, steamfitters need additional training to know how to handle hot liquids and gases. Steamfitters must be certified to do this type of work as well. Like pipe fitters, steamfitters sometimes work on tall buildings that are under construction. Steamfitters usually work for companies that install steam pipe systems in many different buildings, rather than working for an employer in a single building. They may also be on call to fix emergencies on nights or weekends.

What's in the Sprinkler Fitter Study Guide?

The Bureau of Labor Statistics projected that demand for sprinkler fitters would increase as a result of building codes in many states requiring sprinkler systems to be installed in residential and other buildings.

National Testing Inspection and Certification Corporation (NITC) provides certification to the piping industry. The following sample questions are taken from the NITC's 2013 UA Star Mastery Exam Sprinkler Fitter Study Guide.

1. The top of the pipe in an underground installation shall not be less than what depth below the frost line for a locality?
   a. 2 feet
   b. 1 foot *(correct answer)*
   c. 1 ½ feet
   d. ½ foot

2. Which type of piping is no longer permitted to be used as underground supply piping?
   a. Ductile iron
   b. Cast iron *(correct answer)*
   c. Plastic
   d. Cement asbestos

3. You cannot thread which type of piping listed below?
   a. Thin wall schedule 10 *(correct answer)*
   b. Schedule 40 steel pipe
   c. Schedule 40 galvanized
   d. Schedule 30 steel pipe

SPRINKLER FITTERS

Sprinkler fitters install fire protection systems and fix existing systems. Fire protection systems include sprinklers, pipes, and hoses. Some systems use water to put out fires, while others use chemical fire retardants, such as foam.

Sprinkler systems are usually not installed in houses or small apartment buildings. Instead they are installed in buildings like offices, schools, high-rise apartment buildings, restaurants, or manufacturing plants. Some states and cities have a law requiring sprinkler systems to be installed in additional types of buildings, including smaller residential buildings, and more states are likely to introduce this law in the coming years. As a result, sprinkler fitters may have even more work in the next few decades.

WHAT IS A UNION?

A union is a group of workers in the same profession who come together to improve their working situation. For example, teachers or carpenters might form a union. Unions are also sometimes referred to as labor unions or trade unions. Unions try to increase workers' wages or benefits, such as health insurance and retirement plans. Unions also work toward making safety improvements in the industry. They can also help union members if they have problems with an employer.

In North America, many plumbers belong to the United Association of Journeymen and Apprentices of the Plumbing and Pipe Fitting Industry of the United States

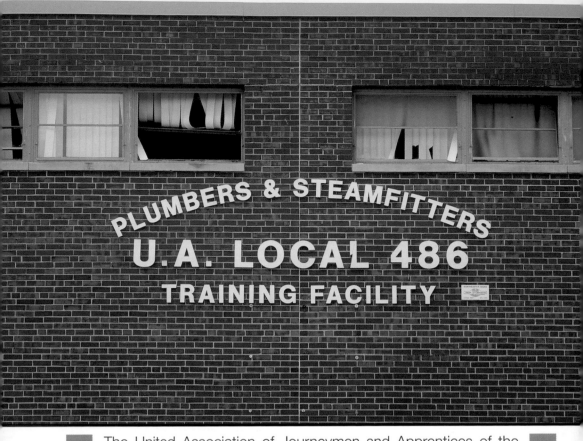

The United Association of Journeymen and Apprentices of the Plumbing and Pipe Fitting Industry, also known as the UA, represents plumbers across North America.

and Canada. This union, which is also known as the UA, is made up of about three hundred smaller local unions. Although plumbers are not usually required to join a union, many find that membership in the UA is beneficial.

Chapter 4

MASTER PLUMBERS AND BUSINESS OWNERS

Licensed plumbers with a good deal of experience in the trade have a number of options when it comes to advancing in the profession. Many experienced plumbers become master plumbers and some go on to start their own plumbing businesses. These positions come with more responsibilities, but they can be very rewarding and come with a bigger salary.

Plumbers who have a great deal of experience in the industry may go on to become project managers. It's important to have good people skills if you are supervising a team of workers.

CAREER PATHS FOR LICENSED PLUMBERS

Once plumbers are licensed, they have several career options. Besides doing the same work they did before, licensed plumbers can also train and supervise other plumbers. For example, a licensed master plumber can train an apprentice or journeyperson plumber. Licensed master plumbers can also become plumbing inspectors. Plumbing inspectors check the work of other plumbers to make sure it meets local plumbing codes.

Licensed plumbers can also become plumbing estimators. Estimators figure out how much time a project will take, what materials are needed, and how much the

If you run your own business as a plumbing contractor, you will be responsible for finding your own clients by advertising and word of mouth.

job will cost. They often work for companies that build large buildings or groups of buildings, such as apartment complexes. Estimators work with engineers and architects before a building project begins.

Plumbers who start their own businesses generally begin by working on their own or with a business partner. As their businesses build, they can hire other people to work for them. In some cases, they might hire additional plumbers to help with the workload or other workers who can offer additional services. For instance, a business owner might hire a person to work on heating or air-conditioning systems or someone who can build or clean septic systems.

Plumbers can also apply their knowledge and expertise to other business pursuits. They might try their hand at starting their own plumbing supply company or starting a company that installs irrigation systems. These types of watering systems might be used on farms to grow crops. Other types of irrigation systems might be set up on residential or business lawns or gardens.

TOOLS OF THE TRADE

A plumber relies on many types of tools to get the job done. The types of tools used vary depending on the project, but most plumbers will have a wide variety of basic tools on hand. Sometimes plumbers will need to transport tools, pipes, and other supplies to the jobsite, so most of them own a truck or a van. Plumbers who run their own businesses will need to own all the necessary tools of the trade.

Q&A with Fred Schilling, Plumber and Entrepreneur

Fred Schilling is the founder and chief operating officer of Pipeline Plumbing in South Florida. After being trained in the plumbing trade while in the Air Force, Schilling became one of Florida's youngest master plumbers ever. As well as running his own business, Schilling is the vice president of Plumbers Without Borders, an organization that connects tradespeople with humanitarian organizations, with the goal of improving health and sanitation across the world. Schilling talked to Andy Orin at *Lifehacker* about running a successful plumbing business:

What misconceptions do people have about plumbing as a job?
They think all we do is unclog sinks and toilets. That it's only a profession for the people who could not go to college.

Is there anything you do differently from your peers in the same profession?
We seek out the most complicated plumbing projects. While many of our fellow plumbers steer clear of complex plumbing problems, we specialize in them.

What kind of things do plumbers do beyond what most people see?
We cover a large geographical area, so we do spend a great deal of time in traffic!

What's the most enjoyable part of the job?
The feeling of accomplishment. I've helped build more than one thousand commercial buildings here in South Florida, so everywhere I go, every day, I see some of them. I am so very proud of them.

Schilling recommends that aspiring plumbers take classes in physics, science, and math. To move up in the trade, he advises plumbers to "get every kind of license and certification you can!"

MEASURING TOOLS

Before plumbers begin jobs, they spend time carefully measuring where pipes will go. Plumbers sometimes use a regular tape measure. For jobs that must be extremely accurate, they generally use a steel rule (a rigid and accurate ruler). Plumbers often mark their measurements with an ordinary pencil or pen, although they might also use a permanent marker to make darker lines that won't wear off. To make markings on sheet metal or metal pipes,

When you work for yourself as a plumber, you will need to own all your own tools. Necessary tools of the trade include saws for cutting piping.

plumbers can use a tool called a scriber. Plumbers use a tool called a center punch to mark the exact center of a circle where a hole will be drilled.

DEMOLITION AND CUTTING TOOLS

For remodeling projects and repairs, plumbers may need to get rid of existing pipes, floors, walls, or ceilings. They might also need to dig out old pipe with a chisel or use pry bars to pull out old or damaged floors or walls.

In the course of a workday, plumbers also use many different types of cutting tools. Tin snips can be used to cut sheet metal. Some types of tin snips can cut curves, while others are better at cutting straight lines. Plumbers often use tubing cutters to cut pipes, although some kinds of pipe require special tools to cut. Copper pipe is generally cut with hacksaws, and chain-link cutters can be used to cut wide cast-iron pipe. The links on chain-link cutters look like a bicycle chain. They can be wrapped around pipes of various sizes. The links are then tightened to cut through the pipe. Plumbers carry wire cutters, as well as a few different types of files. Files are used to smooth the rough edges that are left after metal is cut.

WRENCHES

Plumbers always have many wrenches with them on a job. Wrenches are used to loosen or tighten fasteners, and they also help plumbers get a good grip on a pipe. There are many types of wrenches, including adjustable, basin, pipe, socket, and strap wrenches. Plumbers usually have many wrenches in a variety of sizes.

SOLDERING IRONS AND TORCHES

Plumbers use specialized tools to connect pipe together. One such tool is a soldering iron. Solder is a mixture of metals that melt at a lower temperature than the pipe the plumber wants to join together. Solder comes in wire form or as a bar.

Plumbers use a tool called a soldering iron to heat the solder until it melts. The plumber then applies the melted solder to both halves of a pipe. When the solder cools, it also hardens, and the pipes are securely connected. When using thicker pipes, plumbers use a different tool to melt the solder. This is called a heat torch, which is powered by propane and other types of gases. A heat torch can create much higher temperatures, which are better for melting solder.

PLUNGERS AND AUGERS

To clear blocked pipes and drains, plumbers use plungers and augers. Plungers clear blockages by sucking air and water out of the drain and then forcing it back in. Many households have plungers on hand to clear simple blockages. Augers are flexible tubes with special attachments on the end. A plumber feeds an auger into a blocked pipe. When it reaches the blockage, the plumber twists the attachments to loosen the blockage. Sometimes plumbers attach augers to an electric drill. The drill helps rotate the attachments to exert more force on the blockage.

Many people keep plungers in the bathroom to deal with routine blockages. If that doesn't work, they have to call in a plumber to deal with the problem.

GENERAL AND SAFETY TOOLS

Plumbers carry many common tools that anyone might have for use in his or her home, such as pocketknives, hammers, and screwdrivers. They always have one or two flashlights on hand to see into dark spaces. Plumbers also use mirrors to see around corners when working on jobs where space is limited. On the job, plumbers generally just wear jeans or other long pants and a T-shirt. Since plumbing can be a dirty job, some plumbers wear coveralls to keep their regular clothing clean.

Safety is an important concern for plumbers, and they usually wear eye protection when using cutting tools. They also generally use protective gear, especially protective goggles, when using welding torches. Plumbers protect their hands with gloves when working with sharp metal or hot materials. To protect their feet from falling pipes or tools, they generally wear steel-toed boots. Large construction sites often require all workers, including plumbers, to wear hard hats for their protection.

TYPES OF PIPE

When putting in new pipes in homes, plumbers most often use ones made of copper, plastic, or steel. Residential projects usually don't require a lot of water to flow through pipes. So smaller pipes are generally used for these projects. One or two plumbers or plumber's helpers can install these kinds of pipes.

Plastic pipes are commonly used in residences. There are several types of plastic pipe, including PVC, CPVC, PEX, and PolyPipe. Some of these pipes are used for specialized purposes. For example, PVC is used only for cold water. PolyPipe is often used to connect a house's plumbing system to a city or town water supply, as it is harder than other types of plastic pipe and can carry more water.

Copper pipe is also used in homes. It can carry hot or cold water. In some older homes, galvanized steel was used. If plumbers make repairs to older homes, they must know how to work with galvanized pipe. Today, many plumbers will simply update plumbing systems by replacing galvanized pipe with newer types of pipes. Plumbers also use small tubes for some small jobs. For example, tubing is used to connect an automatic ice maker in a refrigerator to a water supply.

Larger pipes facilitate the movement of larger volumes of water. For instance, the pipes that are used in sewers, or in municipal water supply systems, need to be very large to cope with the amount of fluid that flows through them. These pipes are generally made from cast iron. To install large pipes such as these, plumbers need to work with a team. The team might include experienced pipelayers and pipe fitters. Together, they use machinery to dig trenches for the pipes and to move them. This is specialized work that plumbers need to be trained in.

ATTACHING PIPES

Plumbers use a number of methods to join pipes. Different materials are used to connect different types of pipe. For instance, a plumber can use screws or bolts to connect metal pipes. Metal pipes can also be soldered together. Plastic pipes can be joined by specialized glue.

Many pipes are joined with small devices called fittings. One type of fitting is called a coupling. A coupling is a short length of pipe, usually of the same material as the pipes being attached. Couplings can attach pipes of the same size or pipes that are two different sizes. Other fittings connect more than two pipes. Tees attach three pipes together. They are called tees because they look like the letter "T." They connect two pipes in a straight line and a third pipe perpendicular to the other two. Plumbers use a fitting called a cross to connect four pipes.

Plumbers also use fittings to create a bend in a pipe. These fittings are called elbows, or "ells." Like couplings, they can connect pipes of the same size or of two different sizes. Fittings such as caps and plugs can be put on one end of a pipe to seal it off.

Chapter 5

THE FUTURE OF PLUMBING

The future looks bright for plumbers. Overall job opportunities are expected to be good, and job prospects will be particularly strong for plumbers who keep up to date with new technology being used in the industry. There will also be more and more opportunities for plumbers to install and maintain "green plumbing" technology, as the demand for environmentally sustainable housing and appliances grows. As with most construction trades, employment of plumbers fluctuates with the economy, and plumbers may experience unemployment in times when there is less construction happening. Overall, however, plumbing is a career with a very promising future outlook.

A career as a plumber begins with doing well in school. Plumbers use math and science daily, so it's a good idea to focus on these subjects in high school.

WHAT IS BIM?

Building information modeling (BIM) is the process of generating and managing digital representations of physical systems, including plumbing and drainage systems. BIM technology is used to build three-dimensional models containing all the data for specific water and drainage systems. These models can then be updated automatically when changes need to be made. BIM enables a collaborative way of developing designs for plumbing systems and can help plumbers to create high-quality water supply and drainage systems. According to the Bureau of Labor Statistics, job prospects will be particularly strong for plumbers with knowledge of BIM as the demand for integrated building-planning abilities increases.

OPPORTUNITIES IN GREEN PLUMBING

In the coming years, many houses and buildings will be "going green." Making environmentally friendly improvements in a building's plumbing can save homeowners or business owners money in water or energy costs, and, of course, it also helps the environment by conserving natural resources.

Green plumbers can play a big role in making buildings more energy efficient and environmentally friendly, and there are several types of green changes that plumbers can make in homes and buildings. An example of a simple change is installing high-efficiency fixtures, such as toilets, low-flow showers, and environmentally friendly washing machines. These fixtures and appliances use much less water than older models. For people who are even more

Easy care   On   Cotton

cold   cold
40   40°
60   60
Delicate 30   60 Stains
cold   90
Wool 30   60 Prewash
Drain   Rinse

Spin ⊚

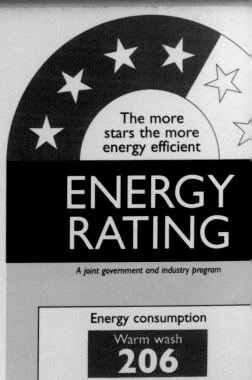

The more stars the more energy efficient

ENERGY RATING

A joint government and industry program

Energy consumption

Warm wash
206

kWh per year
using Cotton 40°C, 900RPM
seven times per week

When tested in accordance with AS/NZS 2040.2.
Actual energy use and running costs will depend on how you use the

All over the world there is an increasing demand for energy-efficient appliances. This is a good thing for the plumbers of the future, who will be required to install these appliances.

serious about greening their building, plumbers can make more extensive changes as well. For instance, they might install radiant heating or solar heating systems, or they may design and install gray water systems.

Plumbers can take courses in green plumbing to add to their set of skills. Trade and vocational schools are adding courses in green technology to their plumbing training programs. Some schools and companies also offer courses for certifying plumbers in green technologies.

HIGH-EFFICIENCY FIXTURES

There have been many advances in green plumbing fixtures. More and more fixtures are being designed to use less water. For example, some newer toilets use much less water than older toilets. These are called low-flow or high-efficiency toilets. Other toilets compost waste, rather than using any water to flush. Some modern urinals actually use no water at all. Front-loading washing machines use much less water than top-loading machines, and modern dishwashers use less water than older models.

HEATING SYSTEMS

Two types of green heating systems rely on plumbing to operate. These are solar heating systems and radiant heating systems. Solar systems use solar energy to generate electricity and to warm water or create electricity. Radiant heat consists of small pipes or tubes that are concealed underneath flooring and carry hot water. This heat radiates upward from the floor. Since radiant heating is so efficient, it costs homeowners less money to heat their building. Sometimes radiant heating is installed in the walls or ceilings of a building as well.

Hattie Hasan: Building an "Army of Women Plumbers"

Hattie Hasan is the founder of Stopcocks, an all-women plumbing company based in the United Kingdom. She started the company in 1990, after deciding to quit her previous job as a teacher. She contacted every plumbing company in the city of Leeds and didn't get a reply from any of them, so she bought her own tools, printed out some flyers advertising her services, and waited for customers to call.

Twenty-eight years later, Stopcocks has female plumbers in cities all over the United Kingdom, and the company is even collaborating with an organization in Kenya to provide clean water with sustainable systems. More than just a plumbing company, it's an organization with a mission. Hasan says she "committed to build an army of women plumbers to change the way water is managed; since it is always women who are impacted by problems with water, whether that is waiting in all day for a plumber who never arrives here in the UK or risking their lives, walking miles carrying water in the developing world."

The main obstacle preventing women from working in plumbing is the lack of interest in the industry, Hasan says. "Many in the industry seem to think that women having a stake and being involved is taking something away from them. Actually it's just us having the right to do it, do it our own way and to have happy customers."

GRAY WATER SYSTEMS

Gray water recycling systems are another popular green plumbing technology. Gray water is wastewater generated by dishwashers, washing machines, sinks, and showers. Gray water can be stored and then reused to water outdoor plants. Sometimes gray water is filtered or processed. It can then be used as water to be flushed in toilets, for example. Plumbers can create and install gray water systems in homes and other buildings.

WOMEN IN PLUMBING

According to 2018 data from the Bureau of Labor Statistics, only 2 percent of plumbers are women. This percentage has increased from 1.5 percent in 2010, but it is clear that women are still underrepresented In the plumbing industry. Chicago Women in Trades executive director Jayne Vellinga believes this is due in part to gender stereotyping about "men's work" and "women's work."

"Gender stereotyping begins at a very early age," Vellinga told Hal Conick for an article in *Contractor* magazine. "Women don't know much about the benefits of the career. It's just not presented as an option to women, either as students or as adult students looking for work." Because women have few role models in plumbing to look up to, they often do not realize that there are great opportunities out there in the plumbing industry. This situation is beginning to change as more women enter the profession.

Other reasons why women don't pursue careers in plumbing include the perception that it is a dirty job and the

Women are underrepresented in the plumbing industry. However, this is changing as more and more women discover what a rewarding career it can be.

perception that it requires a lot of heavy lifting. However, female plumbers generally find that they can handle the physical challenges of the job just as well as men. Susan McDaniel is a plumber who co-owns a plumbing business in North Carolina. In an article in *Plumbing and Mechanical* magazine, she explains that there are ways to approach the physical challenges of the job besides brute force. "I have to use my brain more when I have to lift things. My back isn't as strong, so I have to figure out alternative ways to move heavy items."

It can be helpful for young women who want to be plumbers to try and find a female plumber who works in their area or seek out online communities for women in plumbing. Experienced female plumbers may be willing to discuss the advantages of a career in plumbing or act as a mentor to a novice. Young women should also look for apprenticeship programs that specifically encourage women to apply.

As with many traditionally male occupations, many women find that they face discrimination and harassment just because they are female in the plumbing industry. Profiled in an article in *Reeves Journal* about women in the plumbing industry, plumber Tracy Belvill said, "I put up with insults and intimidation to prove I belonged in this industry." Gender-based discrimination is illegal, and female plumbers and apprentices should report cases of discrimination to the Equal Employment Opportunity Commission or the National Labor Relations Board.

A BRIGHT FUTURE FOR PLUMBERS

No matter whether the economy is good or bad, there will always be opportunities for plumbers. Plumbers provide essential services. They keep showers and toilets working.

Plumbers provide a vital service, and their work will always be needed. If you enjoy solving problems and fixing things, a career as a plumber could be a great choice for you!

They allow water to flow into kitchens and laundry rooms. Plumbers repair broken hot water tanks and sewer lines. Every house, apartment building, school, supermarket, and factory will need a plumber at some time or another. Anyone who likes to make things work, and keep things working, should consider a career as a plumber.

Glossary

APPRENTICESHIP An arrangement in which one person learns a trade from an experienced professional by working alongside that person.

AUGERS Flexible tubes used to clear blockages in pipes.

BLUEPRINT A detailed plan.

BUILDING INFORMATION MODELING The generation and management of digital representations of physical infrastructures such as plumbing systems; known as BIM.

COUPLING A short length of pipe used to attach other pipes together.

CROSS A fitting used to connect four pipes together.

ELBOWS A fitting used to create a bend in a pipe.

FITTING A small device used to connect pipes.

GALVANIZED Pipes that have been coated in zinc to prevent corrosion and rust.

GRAY WATER Wastewater that is stored and reused to reduce the need for clean water.

GREEN PLUMBING Plumbing technology designed to reduce harm to the planet.

JOURNEYPERSON A licensed professional who has completed an apprenticeship and has experience in the trade.

MASTER PLUMBER A licensed professional with extensive experience in the trade.

PIPE FITTER A professional who installs and fixes piping systems in buildings.

PIPELAYER A professional who prepares the area where pipes will go.

SEPTIC TANK A tank in which sewage is treated to remove contaminants.

SOLAR HEATING Heating produced by converting power from sunlight.

SPRINKLER FITTER A professional who installs and fixes fire protection systems.

STEAMFITTER A professional who installs and fixes piping that is used to move water or gas that is under pressure.

TEE A fitting used to connect three pipes together.

UNION A group of workers in the same profession who come together to improve their working situation.

For More Information

American Fire Sprinkler Association (AFSA)
12750 Merit Drive, Suite 350
Dallas, TX 75251
(214) 349-5965
Website: https://www.firesprinkler.org
Facebook: @firesprinkler.org
Twitter: @AFSA
AFSA is a nonprofit organization providing training,
    communication, and advocacy for fire sprinkler
    contractors.

Canadian Institute of Plumbing and Heating (CIPH)
295 The West Mall, Suite 504
Toronto, ON M9C 4Z4
Canada
Website: https://www.ciph.com
Facebook: @CIPH1933
Twitter: @CIPHnews
CIPH is a nonprofit trade organization providing
    advocacy, training, news, and networking
    opportunities for professionals in the plumbing and
    heating industry.

Mechanical Contractors Association of America (MCAA)
1385 Piccard Drive
Rockville, MD 20850
(301) 869-5800
Website: https://www.mcaa.org
Facebook: @MCAAEducation
Twitter: @MCAANews

MCAA provides educational materials and programs to its members in the heating, plumbing, air conditioning, refrigeration, piping, and mechanical industries.

Mechanical Contractors Association of Canada (MCAC)
701-280 Albert Street
Ottawa, ON K1P 5G8
Canada
Website: https://mcac.ca
Facebook: @MechanicalContractorsAssociationofCanada
Twitter: @CANMechanical
MCAC provides business support, advocacy, and resources to its members in Canada's mechanical contracting industry.

National Center for Construction Education and Research (NCCER)
13614 Progress Boulevard
Alachua, FL 32615
(386) 518-6500
Website: https://www.nccer.org/nccer-home
Facebook, Instagram, and Twitter: @NCCER
NCCER is a nonprofit organization that creates standardized curriculum and assessments for workers in the construction trades, with the goal of maintaining a safe and productive workforce.

National Fire Sprinkler Association (NFSA)
514 Progress Drive, Suite A
Linthicum Heights, MD 21090
Website: https://nfsa.org

(443) 863-4464
Facebook: @NFSA.org
Instagram: @NFSA1905
Twitter: @NFSAorg
NFSA is a membership organization providing training, events, and resources for professionals in the fire sprinkler industry.

Plumbing-Heating-Cooling Contractors Association (PHCC)
180 S. Washington Street, Suite 100
Falls Church, VA 22046
(703) 237-8100
Website: https://www.phccweb.org
Facebook: @PHCCNational
Instagram: @NAPHCC
Twitter: @PHCCNatl
PHCC provides education, advocacy, and networking opportunities for professionals in the plumbing, heating, and cooling industry.

United Association of Journeymen and Apprentices of the Plumbing and Pipe Fitting Industry of Canada (UA)
442 Gilmour Street
Ottawa, ON K2P 0RB
Canada
Website: https://www.uacanada.ca
Facebook: @UAcanadamembers
Instagram: @UA.Canada
Twitter: @UACanada

UA Canada is a labor union providing training and advocacy to professionals in the plumbing and piping industry in Canada.

United Association of Journeymen and Apprentices of the Plumbing and Pipe Fitting Industry of the United States (UA)
3 Park Place
Annapolis, MD 21401
(410) 269-2000
Website: http://www.ua.org
Facebook: @UnitedAssociation
Twitter: @UAPipeTrades
UA is a labor union providing training, advocacy, and resources to its members in the plumbing and pipefitting industry across the United States.

For Further Reading

Carosso, Juan. *At Your Best as a Plumber: Your Playbook for Building a Great Career and Launching a Small Business as a Plumber.* New York, NY: Skyhorse Publishing, 2018.

Freedman, Jeri. *Plumber.* New York, NY: Cavendish Square, 2016.

Institute for Career Research. *Careers in Plumbing.* Chicago, IL: Institute for Career Research, 2016.

Kamberg, Mary-Lane. *A Career as a Plumber, Pipefitter, or Steamfitter.* New York, NY: Rosen Publishing, 2019.

Lusted, Marcia Amidon. *Working as a Plumber in Your Community.* New York, NY: Rosen Publishing, 2016.

Morkes, Andrew. *Plumber.* Broomall, PA: Mason Crest, 2019.

Nixon, James, and Bobby Humphrey. *Plumber.* London, UK: Franklin Watts, 2014.

Rose, Simon. *Plumber.* New York, NY: AVW by Weigl, 2016.

Wilkinson, Colin. *Using Math in Construction.* New York, NY: Rosen Publishing, 2018.

Wolny, Philip. *Getting a Job in the Construction Industry.* New York, NY: Rosen Publishing, 2017.

Bibliography

Bureau of Labor Statistics. "Labor Force Statistics from the Current Population Survey." January 19, 2018. https://www.bls.gov/cps/cpsaat11.htm.

Bureau of Labor Statistics. "Plumbers, Pipefitters, and Steamfitters." July 25, 2018. https://www.bls.gov/ooh/construction-and-extraction/plumbers-pipefitters-and-steamfitters.htm.

Conick, Hal. "Why Are There Still So Few Women in Plumbing?" *Contractor*, February 6, 2015. https://www.contractormag.com/plumbing/why-are-there-still-so-few-women-plumbing.

Delose, Mindy. "The Benefits of Building Information Modeling (BIM)." Plumbing Perspective, July 3, 2012. https://plumbingperspective.com/the-benefits-of-building-information-modeling-bim.

Dr. Kit Career Videos. "Pipe Fitter." September 7, 2013. https://www.youtube.com/watch?v=AvaN2chGcCl.

Explore the Trades. "How to Become a Plumber." Career Roadmap. Retrieved November 28, 2018. https://explorethetrades.org/what-we-do/education/plumbing/how-to-become-a-plumber.

Faloon, Kelly, and Katie Rotella. "Women in Plumbing: Where Are They? The Plumbing Industry Is Experiencing a Labor Shortage. So Why Not Hire Women?" *Plumbing & Mechanical*, November 1, 2002.

Levine, Wendy. "Women in the Plumbing Industry." *Reeves Journal*, March 12, 2008. https://www.reevesjournal.com/articles/85423-women-in-the-plumbing-industry.

Lynch, Amy. "Hot Job: Future for Plumbers Is No Pipe Dream." *Indy Star*, January 10, 2018. https://www

.indystar.com/story/money/2015/01/10/hot-job
-future-plumbers-pipe-dream/21357143.

Maiden, Beth. "Follow Your Arrow: Hattie Hasan and
Her Army of Female Tradespeople." Autostraddle,
January 28, 2016. https://www.autostraddle.com
/follow-your-arrow-queer-plumber-hattie-hasan-and
-her-army-of-female-tradespeople-324605.

McKay, Dawn Rosenberg. "Everything You Need
to Know About Being a Plumber." The Balance
Careers, May 12, 2018. https://www
.thebalancecareers.com/plumber-job-description
-and-duties-4107383.

National Fire Protection Association. "Sprinkler
Requirements." Retrieved October 11, 2018. https://
www.nfpa.org/Public-Education/Campaigns/Fire
-Sprinkler-Initiative/Legislation-and-adoptions
/Sprinkler-requirements.

Olexiuk, Andrew. "3 Ridiculous Plumbing Stories You
Won't Believe." Absolute Draining and Plumbing,
June 22, 2016. https://www.absolutedp
.com/2016/3-ridiculous-plumbing-stories-you-wont
-believe.

Orin, Andy. "Career Spotlight: What I Do as a Plumber."
Lifehacker, February 24, 2016. https://lifehacker
.com/career-spotlight-what-i-do-as-a
-plumber-1760572480.

Owano, Mickey. "The Latest Trends in Smart Plumbing
Technology." Tritan Plumbing, December 19, 2016.
https://www.tritan-plumbing.com/blog/latest-trends
-smart-plumbing-technology.

PopMech Editors. "7 Nightmarish Plumber Horror Stories." *Popular Mechanics*, April 25, 2017. https://www.popularmechanics.com/home/interior-projects/a26202/7-plumbing-horror-stories.

Stopcocks Women Plumbers. "An Introduction to Stopcocks." Retrieved October 11, 2018. stopcocks.uk/about/an-introduction-to-stopcocks.

Stutz, Billy. "How to Become a Professional Plumber." Ferguson, February 28, 2017. https://www.ferguson.com/content/trade-talk/business-tips/how-to-become-a-plumber.

United Association of Plumbers, Fitters, Welders, and Service Techs. "Overview." Retrieved October 11, 2018. http://www.ua.org/overview.

US News & World Report. "How Much Do Plumbers Make?" Retrieved October 11, 2018. https://money.usnews.com/careers/best-jobs/plumber/salary.

Wisler, James. "Pros and Cons of Careers in the Plumbing Industry." Wisler Plumbing, April 17, 2018. https://www.wislerplumbing.com/pros-cons-of-careers-in-the-plumbing-industry.

A

appliance, 11, 28, 30, 57, 59
apprentice, 12, 16, 18–19, 39, 46, 65
  additional skills, 23
  requirements, 21–22, 33
  wages and benefits, 22
architect, 28, 47

B

blueprint, 15, 19, 22, 24, 28

C

chemical, 28, 41, 43
code
  building, 19, 24, 30, 42
  plumbing, 15, 33, 35, 46
construction, 8, 10, 15, 25–26, 28, 33, 41, 54, 57
contractor, 10, 21–23, 28

E

education
  community college, 14–16, 18–19
  General Education Development (GED), 15, 21
  guidance counselor, 14, 18–19
  high school, 8, 12, 14–16, 18, 21
  Job Corps, 15
  technical school, 14–16, 18
  vocational (or trade) school, 12, 14–16, 18–19, 36, 61
estimator, 46–47

F

fixture, 10–12, 28, 30, 32–33, 35, 59, 61

G

gray water system, 61, 63
green plumbing, 57, 59, 61, 63

H

Hasan, Hattie, 7–8, 62
heating system, 11, 26, 39, 41, 61
high-efficiency fixture, 59, 61

I

installation, 28, 42
irrigation system, 48

J

Job Corps, 15
journeyperson, 33, 46

M

McDaniel, Susan, 65
Mechanical Contractors
    Association of
    America, 22

N

National Fire Sprinkler
    Association, 22
National Testing Inspection
    and Certification
    Corporation (NITC), 42
natural gas, 10–12, 22

P

pipe
    attaching, 30, 32–33, 38,
        55–56
    fitting, 9, 22, 39, 43, 56
    steam, 26, 41
    system, 22, 28, 38–39
    types of, 19, 28, 35,
        54–56
pipe fitter, 8, 10, 12, 37,
    39, 41, 55
pipelayer, 37–38, 55

plumber
    business owner, 18, 23,
        45, 47–49, 59, 65
    career paths, 6–8, 12,
        14–15, 37, 39, 46–48,
        57, 63, 65–66
    certification, 21, 42, 49
    education and, 8, 12,
        14–16, 18–19, 21, 36, 61
    exam, 33, 35–36, 42
    general, 24–26, 28–30,
        32–33, 35–36, 37
    general statistics, 8,
        10–12, 42, 59, 63
    getting a license, 33,
        35–36
    job description, 6–8,
        9–12
    job growth, and
        employment, 6–8,
        9–10, 22, 49, 57, 59,
        61–63, 65–66
    licensed, 19, 33, 46–48
    master, 8, 19, 33, 45–
        46, 49
    math, and science skills,
        12, 14, 22, 39, 49
    "on call" emergencies, 8,
        24, 41
    self-employed
        plumbers, 10

union, 21–22, 43–44
wages, and benefits, 10,
    16, 22, 33, 43–44, 45,
    63
welding, 14–15, 22, 26,
    38, 54
women, 7–8, 62–63, 65
workload of, 12, 24–26,
    28–30, 32–33, 47
Plumbers Without Borders,
    49
plumbing
commercial, 10, 23, 28,
    49
residential, 8, 10, 23, 28,
    33, 42–43, 48, 54
Plumbing-Heating-
    Cooling Contractors
    Association, 22

S
safety, 16, 22, 26, 43, 54
Schilling, Fred, 8, 48–49
septic system, 11, 28, 47
sewage line, or system, 11,
    28, 32, 35, 55, 66
solar heating system, 61
sprinkler fitter, 8, 37,
    42–43
steamfitter, 8, 10, 37, 41

T
tools, 7, 14, 19, 22, 48–
    52, 54
demolition, and cutting,
    30, 50–51, 54
general, and safety, 19, 54
measuring, 30, 50–51
plunger, and auger, 29, 52
safety, 19, 54
soldering iron, and torch,
    26, 52, 54
trap, and vent, 29, 32
wrench, 51

U
unions, and organizations,
    21–22, 43–44
United Association of
    Journeymen and
    Apprentices of the
    Plumbing and Pipe
    Fitting Industry of the
    United States and
    Canada (UA), 22, 42,
    43–44
US Department of Labor, 15

V
Vellinga, Jayne, 63

ABOUT THE AUTHORS

Rachel Given-Wilson has written and edited many nonfiction books for teenagers, including the Tech Girls series of books about careers for girls in STEM industries. She lives in Brooklyn with her family.

Simone Payment has a degree in psychology from Cornell University and a master's degree in elementary education from Wheelock College. She is the author of numerous books for young adults. Her book *Inside Special Operations: Navy SEALs* (also from Rosen Publishing) won a 2004 Quick Picks for Reluctant Young Adult Readers award from the American Library Association and is on the Nonfiction Honor List of Voice of Youth Advocates.

PHOTO CREDITS

Cover SpeedKingz/Shutterstock.com; back cover, pp. 6–7, interior pages (background) asadykov/Shutterstock.com; p. 7 (inset) Nor Gal /Shutterstock.com; p. 11 kurhan/Shutterstock.com; p. 13 Miles Studio /Shutterstock.com; pp. 16–17 grafvision/Shutterstock.com; pp. 20–21 goodluz/Shutterstock.com; p. 25 IanRedding/Shutterstock.com; pp. 26–27 Narin Eungsuwat/Shutterstock.com; pp. 30–31 Jovica Varga/Shutterstock.com; pp. 34–35 Image Source /Getty Images; p. 38 William Taufic/Corbis/Getty Images; p. 40 Ray Ives/Gallo Images/Getty Images; p. 44 Patrick Smith /Getty Images; p. 46 anandaBGD/E+/Getty Images; p. 47 David J. Green/Alamy Stock Photo; p. 50 JooFotia/Shutterstock.com; p. 53 Jon Schulte/Shutterstock.com; p. 58 Roy Mehta/Iconica /Getty Images; p. 60 Eco Images/Universal Images Group /Getty Images; p. 64 Construction Photography/Avalon/Hulton Archive/Getty Images; p. 66 Alexander Raths/Shutterstock.com.

Design and Layout: Nicole Russo-Duca; Photo Researcher: Sherri Jackson